Reading for Today

A Sequential **2** Program for Adults

Program Authors	Jim Beers
	Linda Beech
	Tara McCarthy
	Sam V. Dauzat
	Jo Ann Dauzat
Teacher's Edition Author	Norman Najimy
Program Consultant	Donna Amstutz
Program Advisors	Lonnie Farrell
	Aryola Taylor
	Adriana Figueroa
	Carol Paggi
	Jean Batey
	Ann Reed
	Sharon Darling
	Susan Paull

STECK-VAUGHN COMPANY
AUSTIN, TEXAS
A Division of National Education Corporation

Acknowledgements

Design and Production:
Visual Education Corporation, Princeton, New Jersey

Photography:
Jim Myers—cover
Rick Patrick—iv–1,9,10,11,25,26,33,34,35,62,72–73,82
Kurt Johnson—iv (inset), 2,12–13,24,46,81
Sandy Wilson—21,22,23,36–37,38,45,47
Mike Flahive—48–49,50,57,58,59
Ziggy Kaluzny—60–61,69,70,71
The Picture Store—13 (inset)
The Picture Cube—14
Bob Daemmrich/TexaStock—74
The Picture Cube/Ellis Herwig—83

ISBN: 0-8114-1903-7

67890 VP 90

Table of Contents

Big Money for the Key Family

I can buy a store.

I can use the money to pay that big bill.

We can buy a home.

We can get a car and a van.

Review Words

A. Check the words you know.

1. big   2. bill   3. buy

4. can   5. family   6. home

7. money   8. pay   9. stop

10. store   11. use   12. work

B. Read the sentence.

The family can stop at the store.

C. Write these sentences.

1. The family can stop at the store.
   The _____

2. I can use the money to pay a bill.
   _____

3. We can work to buy a home.
   _____

4. We have a big family.
   _____

Sight Words

lucky   ticket

▶ The Key family can buy a <u>lucky</u> <u>ticket</u>.

A. Read the words in color. Read the example sentence. Underline the new words in sentences 1 and 2 below.

1. The ticket can pay money.

2. The Key family is lucky.

B. Draw lines to match the words.

lucky   TICKET

ticket   LUCKY

C. Write the words below in the sentences.

ticket   lucky

1. You can buy a t‌i‌_ _ _ _ _ at the store.

2. The Key family has a l_ _ _ _ ticket.

D. Write the sentence.

The Key family can buy a lucky ticket.

_____

Sight Words

win   lose   on

▶ You can <u>win</u>, and you can <u>lose</u> money <u>on</u> a ticket.

A. Read the words in color. Read the example sentence. Underline the new words in sentences 1–4 below.

1. You are lucky to win.

2. You can buy a home with the money you win.

3. You can lose money on a ticket.

4. It is not lucky to lose money.

B. Write the words in the boxes.

win | W | |

lose | | | |

on | | |

C. Write the words below in the sentences.

win   lose   on

1. I am lucky. This ticket can w＿＿.

2. Are you lucky? No, this ticket can l＿＿＿.

3. You can lose money o＿ a ticket.

D. Write the sentence.

You can win, and you can lose money on a ticket.

Sight Words

hat   chance

▶ You have a **chance** to win a **hat**.

A. Read the words in color.   Read the example sentence.   Underline the new words in sentences 1–4 below.

1. A ticket is a chance to win money.

2. It is a big chance to lose money.

3. I am lucky. I can win a hat.

4. No, you have a big chance to lose.

B. Write the two new words into the puzzle.

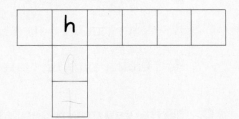

C. Write the words below in the sentences.

chance   hat

1. You have a c＿＿＿＿＿ to win.   You are lucky.

2. You can buy a big home and a big h＿＿.

D. Write the sentence.

You have a chance to win a hat.

Phonics: Short a
—an
can

can

fan

man

pan

A. Read the words in color.
Make other —an words below.

b + an = _____ban_____

r + an = _____

t + an = _____

v + an = _____

B. Read the sentences. Circle the words with —an
and write them.

1. (Dan) is a (man) _____Dan_____   _____man_____

2. He (can) sit by a big (fan). _____   _____

3. The (fan) is not working well. _____

4. Get a (pan) of water for (Dan). _____   _____

C. Write your own sentence.
Use an —an word.

_____

_____

D. Write the —an words.

can		

Phonics: Short a
—at
hat

hat
bat
cat
fat

A. **Read the words in color.**
Make other —at words below.

m + at = _____

p + at = _____

r + at = _____

s + at = _____

B. **Read the sentences. Circle the words**
with —at and write them.

1. Pat has a lucky ticket from Dan._____

2. She has a chance to win a cat._____

3. Jan has money to buy a hat._____

4. She can buy a bat for Dan at the store._____

C. **Write your own sentence.**
Use an —at word.

_____

_____

D. **Write the —at words.**

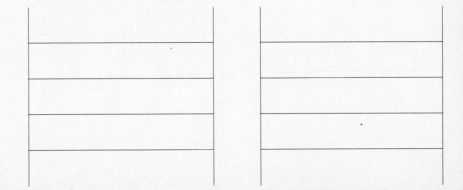

Making Plurals

bill + s = bills

A. Write the plural word.

1. home ___homes___   2. chance _____

3. store _____   4. van _____

5. ticket _____   6. Key _____

B. Practice reading the sentences.

The Keys pay the bills at the stores.
They stop to buy ten tickets.   They can win
two vans with two lucky tickets.   Are the chances
to win big?

C. Read these words. Then write one of the words in each sentence.

Keys   tickets   vans   chances

1. The K_e_y_s_ pay the bills at the stores.

2. They stop to buy ten t_____

3. They can win two v___ with two lucky

   tickets.

4. Are the c_____ to win big?

Is He Lucky?

Dan: This is the lucky ticket, Jan.

Pat: No, it is not lucky.

Dan: It is lucky for us, not for you.

Jan: We have bills to pay, Dan.
        We do not have money for tickets.

—Lucky—

Dan: A family <u>can</u> win!
The Keys have money from a ticket.

Pat: The Keys are lucky.
The chance to win is not big.
The chance to lose <u>is</u> big!

Dan: You can not stop me.
Both Jan and I are lucky to have this ticket.
We can buy a van with the money we win
from this!

–Lucky–

Pat: Dan is going to lose money.
He can lose <u>big</u> money.
He ran to the store to buy two tickets.

Jan: He can use work, not tickets.

Pat: Dan can not win with two tickets.
He buys and buys.
He can not stop.
You can lose money on Dan.

Jan: The chances are big that he can lose <u>me</u>!

Think About It

1. Where did Dan go? Why?
2. Is Jan mad at Dan? Why?

From Home to Home

I can not get work in the country.
I have to go to the city to get a job.
Can I get by in the city?

Review Words

A. Check the words you know.

☐ 1. bus   ☐ 2. by   ☐ 3. city

☐ 4. country   ☐ 5. get   ☐ 6. go

☐ 7. help   ☐ 8. her   ☐ 9. job

☐ 10. not   ☐ 11. three   ☐ 12. work

B. Read the sentence.

Can I get a job in the city?

C. Write these sentences.

1. Can I get a job in the city?

   _____

2. I can not get work in the country.

   _____

3. I can go by bus to the city.

   _____

4. I can get help from the family.

   _____

5. Three of her family like the city.

   _____

Sight Words

my	got	make

▶ <u>My</u> family is in the country.
I <u>got</u> a job to <u>make</u> money.

A. Read the words in color. Read the example sentences. Underline the new words in sentences 1–3.

1. The country was my home.

2. I got a job in the city.

3. Can I make money at a store?

B. Draw lines to match the words.

my   GOT

got   MAKE

make   MY

C. Write the words below in the sentences.

got   make   my

1. I g__ a chance to work in the city.

2. I can m___ money at the store.

3. My pay can help me get m_ family to the city.

D. Write the sentences.

1. My family is in the country.

_____

2. I got a job to make money.

_____

Sight Words

children   mother   send

▶ I <u>send</u> money to my <u>mother</u> for my <u>children</u>.

A. Read the words in color. Read the example sentence. Underline the new words in sentences 1–3.

1. Both my mother and my children are in the country.

2. I send them money from my pay.

3. I am lucky to have my mother with my children.

B. Write the words in the boxes.

mother

send

children

C. Write the words below in the sentences.

children   mother   send

1. I have three c_____.

2. My m_____ is a big help to me.

3. She can use the money I s____ her.

D. Write the sentence.

I send money to my mother for my children.

Sight Words

will	love	went

▶ I love my children and will help them.
I went to work for them.

A. Read the words in color. Read the example sentences. Underline the new words in sentences 1–3.

1. I went to get three bus tickets.

2. I will send them to my children.

3. My mother is well and sends her love to me.

B. Look down and across. Find the words in the box. Circle them.

will

love

went

```
t d w c q v l
w e n t r e o
s q r e f r v
a w i l l x e
```

C. Write the words below in the sentences.

went   love   will

1. My mother w___ to the bus stop with us.

2. My children l___ her.

3. I w___ buy a bus ticket and send it to her.

D. Write the sentences.

1. I love my children and will help them.

_____

2. I went to work for them.

_____

Phonics: Short e
—end
send

send

bend

end

A. Read the words in color.
   Make other —end words below.

l + end = _____

m + end = _____

t + end = _____

B. Read the sentences. Circle the words with —end and write them.

1. My mother is in the city to tend my children.

   _____

2. The family will lend me money to pay the

   bills. _____

3. I send my love to my family. _____

4. This family will win in the end. _____

5. I will sit by the light to mend my hat. _____

C. Write your own sentence.
   Use an —end word.

_____

_____

D. Write the —end words.

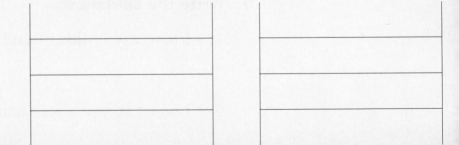

Phonics: Short e
—ent
w**ent**

went
rent
sent
tent

A. Read the words in color.
Make other —ent words below.

b + ent = _____

d + ent = _____

l + ent = _____

B. Read the sentences. Circle the words with —ent
and write them.

1. I rent my home. _____

2. My car has a dent in it. _____

3. My mother went to the country. _____

4. Mother sent her love to my children. _____

5. I can not use this zipper; it is bent. _____

C. Write your own sentence.
Use an —ent word.

_____

_____

D. Write the —ent words.

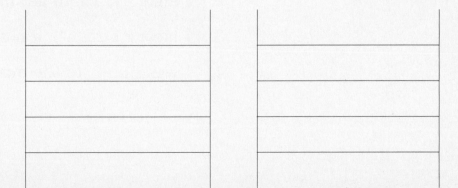

Adding −s, −ed, and −ing to Verbs

help + s = helps   help + ed = helped
help + ing = helping

A. Add the ending.
Write each new word.

		Add −s:	Add −ed:	Add −ing:
1.	work	works	worked	working
2.	tend	_____	_____	_____
3.	walk	_____	_____	_____
4.	look	_____	_____	_____
5.	rent	_____	_____	_____

B. Practice reading the sentences.

I am working in the city. I am tending my children. I am going to get help from my mother.
I have rented a home. I have looked for a job. I walked to the bus stop to get to work. It looks to me like this family is going to make it.

C. Read these words. Then write one of the words in each sentence.

rented   tending   walked   going

1. I am t_____ my children.

2. I am g_____ to get help from my mother.

3. I have r_____ a home.

4. I w_____ to the bus stop to get to work.

A Ticket Home

My mother is with my family
in the city.   She is helping me tend
my three children.   This is not working for her.
She loves her country home.   I got her a
bus ticket, and she is going home.

—Home—

My mother went home to the country.
She was a big help to me. Her help has ended.
The children and I will have to get by. I have
my job, and I will tend my children.
The city is my home.

—Home—

My children are in the city and my mother is in the country. Will my children lose her love? Not a chance! Lucky children! I am sending them to my mother in the country. I can use the money that I make at my job. My children will have both a city home and a country home. The love in this family will make us win in the end.

Think About It

1. Who went home on the bus?
2. Will the children get to see her? How?

Can I Stop?

Van: Look at this!
       This will not work for me.
       I can not stop.

Pat: You <u>can</u> stop.
       People like you can get help.
       It pays to stop.

Van: I am sick of this.
       I am going to get help.

Review Words

A. Check the words you know.

☐ 1. chance   ☐ 2. have   ☐ 3. help

☐ 4. like   ☐ 5. lucky ☐ 6. me

☐ 7. of   ☐ 8. pay   ☐ 9. people

☐ 10. sick   ☐ 11. stop   ☐ 12. that

B. Read the sentence.

People like me have to have help to stop.

C. Write these sentences.

1. I can get sick from this.

_____

2. One of my sisters will pay for me to get help.

_____

3. I am lucky to have a chance to stop.

_____

4. That help will make me stop.

_____

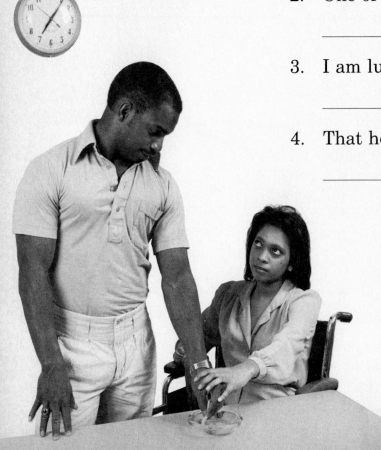

Sight Words

smoke   smoking   do

▶ <u>Do</u> you <u>smoke</u>?
I will work to stop <u>smoking</u>.

A. **Read the words in color. Read the example sentences. Underline the new words in sentences 1—4.**

1. They will ban smoking on the job.

2. I can not smoke at work.

3. Do people like me have a chance to stop?

4. I will stop smoking with help.

B. **Copy the words.**

1. | DO NOT SMOKE | _____ _____ _____

2. | NO SMOKING | _____ _____

C. **Write the words below in the sentences.**

smoking   smoke   Do

1. Pat can help me stop s_____.

2. I s_____, and I will pay for it.

3. D_ people get sick from smoking?

D. **Write the sentences.**

1. Do you smoke?

   _____

2. I will work to stop smoking.

   _____

Sight Words

health   bet   group

▶ **I bet that this health group can help me.**

A. Read the words in color. Read the example sentence. Underline the new words in sentences 1–4.

1. The group helps people to stop smoking.

2. I bet it is a job to work with a group.

3. I bet it is a job to stop smoking.

4. I will work for my health.

B. Write the words in the boxes.

health

bet

group

C. Write the words below in the sentences.

group   health   bet

1. I like to work in a g_ _ _ _ _

2. I went to a big h_ _ _ _ _ _ group that has nine people in it.

3. I b_ _ the group can help me stop smoking.

D. Write the sentence.

I bet that this health group can help me.

Sight Words

ad   **feel**   **out**

▶ **The <u>ad</u> makes me <u>feel</u> "<u>out</u> of it."**

A. Read the words in color.   Read the example sentence.   Underline the new words in sentences 1—4.

1.   I feel that I can stop smoking.

2.   The ad is for people like me.

3.   I will get out of the group that smokes.

4.   The ad makes people feel that they can do it.

B. Look down and across.   Find the words in the box. Circle them.

ad

feel

out

w	o	q	n	s	h	y
k	u	x	a	d	r	v
j	t	p	f	e	e	l
b	x	e	g	c	m	p

C. Write the words below in the sentences.

out   feel   ad

1.   I will go o＿＿ for a walk.

2.   I f＿＿＿ that this walk will help my health.

3.   I feel that the stop-smoking a＿ helps people.

D. Write the sentence.

The ad makes me feel "out of it."

_____

Phonics: Short a
—ad
ad

---

ad

bad

dad

sad

A. **Read the words in color.**
Make other —ad words below.

f + ad = _____

h + ad = _____

m + ad = _____

p + ad = _____

B. **Read the sentences. Circle the words with —ad and write them.**

1. I feel sad that I am smoking. _____

2. Smoking is bad for my health. _____

3. I get mad and yell at my children. _____

4. Smoking is a fad. _____

C. **Write your own sentence.**
Use an —ad word.

_____

_____

D. **Write the —ad words.**

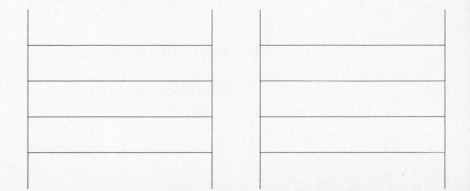

Phonics: Short e
—et
bet

---

bet

get

let

set

A. **Read the words in color.**
Make other —et words below.

j + et = _____   w + et = _____

m + et = _____   y + et = _____

p + et = _____

B. **Read the sentences. Circle the words with —et and write them.**

1. I bet you that I can stop smoking. _____

2. I met a group of people that I like. _____

3. The group will get me to stop. _____

4. I have not ended my smoking yet. _____

5. They do not let me smoke at work. _____

C. **Write your own sentence.**
Use an —et word.

_____

_____

D. **Write the —et words.**

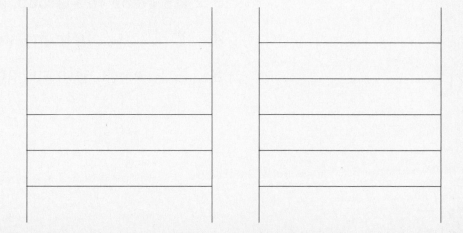

Using Contractions

$$\text{I } \cancel{am} = \text{I'm}$$

A. Read the contractions and write them.

1. I $\cancel{will}$ = I'll

   _I'll_

2. it $\cancel{is}$ = it's

   _____

3. they $\cancel{will}$ = they'll

   _____

4. can $\cancel{not}$ = can't

   _____

B. Practice reading the sentences.

I'm sick of smoking.   I'm going to stop.
I can't smoke on the job.   I'm going to a group,
and it's helping me.   I'll work with the group.
They'll help me stop.

C. Read these words.   Then write one of the words in each sentence.

can't   I'm   it's   they'll   I'll

1. I c_an't_ smoke on the job.

2. I'_ sick of smoking.

3. I'm going to a group, and i_ _ helping me.

4. T_ _ _ _ _ _ help me stop smoking.

5. I'_ _ work with the group.

Help From the Group

I have to stop smoking!
This group helps me feel
like I can do it.
I'm lucky to get this chance
to end my smoking.

I was feeling "out of it,"
out of the group. Smoking was
a ticket to feeling <u>in</u>,
like people in the ads.
I'll bet that this group
can help me stop.

–Help–

I like to smoke, yet smoking can make me sick. It's bad for my health. I'll pay for my smoking, both with money and with bad health.

They are going to ban smoking on my job, and I can't smoke at work. My family will not let me smoke at home. I'll stop smoking! I can do it!

—Help—

    My family is lucky that I got help.
My children like a home with no smoke.
And they can't stand smoke in the car.
I'm lucky that I got in that health group!

Think About It

1. What helped Van stop smoking?
2. Why did Van quit smoking?

With the Family

I have set the table. My sisters are helping me with the food. My brother is looking out for the children. Bill went out in the car to get my mother. I'm lucky to have a big family like this.

Review Words

A. Check the words you know.

- ☐ 1. brother
- ☐ 2. car
- ☐ 3. children
- ☐ 4. family
- ☐ 5. food
- ☐ 6. mother
- ☐ 7. sister
- ☐ 8. table
- ☐ 9. two
- ☐ 10. us
- ☐ 11. was
- ☐ 12. with

B. Read the sentence.

Mother has food for the family table.

C. Write these sentences.

1. Mother has food for the family table.

   _____

2. My brother was standing by the children.

   _____

3. Both of us went to get Mother in the car.

   _____

4. My two sisters help me with the food.

   _____

Sight Words

our	holiday	be

▶ **This will <u>be</u> a big <u>holiday</u> for <u>our</u> family.**

A. **Read the words in color. Read the example sentence. Underline the new words in sentences 1—4.**

1. Our family loves a holiday.

2. I like to be with them.

3. My sisters will be with me for the holiday.

4. We will have a group of eight in our home for this holiday.

B. **Draw lines to match the words.**

our   HOLIDAY

holiday   BE

be   OUR

C. **Write the new words below in the sentences.**

holiday	our	be

1. The children love h———— food.

2. The children in o—— family help with the work.

3. They'll b— at the table with us.

D. **Write the sentence.**

This will be a big holiday for our family.

Sight Words

some   talk   eat

▶ We <u>talk</u> and <u>eat</u> <u>some</u> food at the table.

A. Read the words in color.   Read the example sentence.   Underline the new words in sentences 1–4.

1.   We eat well on holidays.

2.   I'll have a chance to talk with my two sisters.

3.   Some of our talks help me.

4.   My brother and I eat and do some talking.

B. Write the three new words into the puzzle.

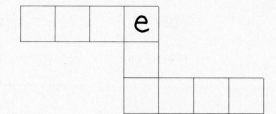

C. Write the words below in the sentences.

talk   some   eat

1.   We will not t___ with my brother Dan.

2.   We will not have a chance to e__ with him.

3.   S___ of our family can not be with us.

D. Write the sentence.

We talk and eat some food at the table.

Sight Words

fed	good	top

▶ I set the food on <u>top</u> of the table.
I <u>fed</u> my family <u>good</u> food.

A. **Read the words in color.   Read the example sentences.   Underline the new words in sentences 1—4.**

1.   It was a good holiday.

2.   I fed my family good food.

3.   I set a pan on top of a mat.

4.   Can we top this holiday?

B. **Write the words in the boxes.**

top

good

fed

C. **Write the words below in the sentences.**

top   good   fed

1.   The t＿＿ of the pan was bent.

2.   I went to the store to get a g＿＿＿ pan.

3.   I f＿＿ my family at the table.

D. **Write the sentences.**

1.   I set the food on top of the table.

_____

2.   I fed my family good food.

_____

Phonics: Short o
—op
top

top
cop
hop
pop

A. Read the words in color.
Make other —op words below.

$m + op = $ _____

$st + op = $ _____

B. Read the sentences. Circle the words with —op and write them.

1. Mother set the holiday food on top of the
   table. _____

2. The children hop to the table. _____

3. I'm good with a mop. _____

4. My brother is a good cop. _____

5. He will buy a can of pop at the store. _____

C. Write your own sentence.
Use an —op word.

_____

_____

D. Write the —op words.

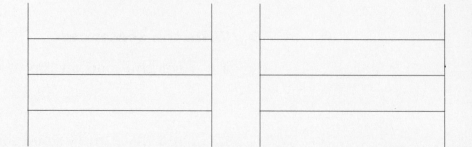

Phonics: Short e
—ed
fed

fed
bed
led
red
wed

A. Read the words in color.
   Make other —ed words below.

J + ed = _____

N + ed = _____

T + ed = _____

B. Read the sentences. Circle the words with —ed
   and write them.

1. I fed the dog some pet food. _____

2. Ted had a good holiday with us. _____

3. We led our children to the table. _____

4. I'll stop the car at the red light. _____

5. We do not eat in bed. _____

C. Write your own sentence.
   Use an —ed word.

_____

_____

D. Write the —ed words.

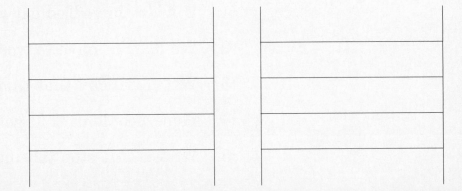

Using Contractions

I have = I've   **do not = don't**

A. Read the contractions and write them.

1. we will = we'll

2. was not = wasn't

3. we are = we're

4. can not = can't

5. is not = isn't

6. will not = won't

B. Practice reading the sentences.

We're lucky that this holiday is the tops for us. Some people can't get home for the holiday. They have to work. We don't have to work this holiday. We'll talk and talk. We won't stop talking to eat. We'll have Ted eat with our family.

C. Read these words. Then write one of the words in each sentence.

we'll   don't   we're   can't   won't

1. We'll have Ted eat with our family.

2. We d___ have to work this holiday.

3. W___ lucky that this holiday is the tops.

4. Some people c___ get home for the holiday.

5. We w___ stop talking to eat.

Our Holiday

Our family had a good holiday. My two sisters helped me get the food on the table. My brother helped us with the children. We had a good chance to be with our mother and talk. Our holiday was the tops.

–Holiday–

One of my brothers is a cop.
He is in our family, yet he can't be home.
He worked on the holiday. He had to eat
out on the job. He wasn't with us.

–Holiday–

Our family likes to help people on holidays. We send food to some people in bad health. We have people in for food and a chance to talk.

Ted was with our family for the holiday. He can't get out to the country to be with family. We went to get Ted in our car. We fed him and helped him feel at home with us.

Our holiday was the tops. We had a chance to help some people. We get a good feeling from this. It's work we love to do. We won't stop.

Think About It

1. Who had to work on the holiday?
2. Why was Ted with this family?

WOMAN LOSES RADIO AND TV

Cops Get Man on the Run

Review Words

A. Check the words you know.

☐ 1. at   ☐ 2. can't   ☐ 3. don't

☐ 4. job   ☐ 5. look   ☐ 6. loses

☐ 7. man   ☐ 8. radio   ☐ 9. run

☐ 10. talk   ☐ 11. they   ☐ 12. woman

B. Read the sentence.

It's that man. He got my radio and TV.

C. Write these sentences.

1. It's that man. He got my radio and TV.

_____

2. Don't let that woman run to the cops.

_____

3. A woman loses her radio, and the cops look for it.

_____

4. They can't talk to me like that.

_____

5. This woman has a job at a store.

_____

Sight Words

trouble	mistake	wrong

▶ I got in <u>trouble</u> by <u>mistake</u>.
That woman is <u>wrong</u>.

A. **Read the words in color. Read the example sentences. Underline the new words in sentences 1–3.**

1. I'm in big trouble.

2. They got the wrong man.

3. It's her mistake, yet they feel I'm the one.

B. **Draw lines to match the words.**

mistake   WRONG

trouble   MISTAKE

wrong   TROUBLE

C. **Write the words below in the sentences.**

mistakes   wrong   trouble

1. People do make m_____.

2. The woman led the cops to the w_____ man.

3. This t_____ will make me lose my job.

D. **Write the sentences.**

1. I got in trouble by mistake.

   _____

2. That woman is wrong.

   _____

Sight Words

arrested   but   law

▶ They <u>arrested</u> me, <u>but</u> the <u>law</u> will help me.

A. **Read the words in color. Read the example sentence. Underline the new words in sentences 1–3.**

 1. I was arrested by the home of that woman.

 2. I was working by her home, but I wasn't in it.

 3. The law can work for me, but will I win?

B. **Write the three new words into the puzzle.**

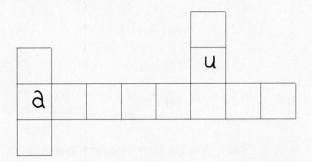

C. **Write the words below in the sentences.**

law   but   arrested

 1. The l＿＿ will help me.

 2. I feel bad, b＿＿ I've sent for some help.

 3. I was a＿＿＿＿＿＿＿ by mistake.

D. **Write the sentence.**

They arrested me, but the law will help me.

Sight Words

hand   **about**   **time**

▶ It's <u>about</u> <u>time</u> for me to get a helping <u>hand</u>.

A. Read the words in color. Read the example sentence. Underline the new words in sentences 1–4.

1. I talked about my chances with Ned.

2. He has the job well in hand.

3. He can get me out in time for the holidays.

4. I won't do time for this.

B. Look down and across. Find the words in the box. Circle them.

hand

about

time

```
v a b o u t i
c p k w l i s
h a n d q m l
b r c f x e j
```

C. Write the words below in the sentences.

time   about   hands

1. I've had a bad t ＿ ＿ ＿ .

2. That woman is wrong a ＿ ＿ ＿ ＿ me.

3. I'm in the h ＿ ＿ ＿ ＿ of the law.

D. Write the sentence.

It's about time for me to get a helping hand.

Phonics: Short u
—ut
but

but

cut

rut

A. **Read the words in color.**
Make other —ut words below.

g + ut = _____

n + ut = _____

B. **Read the sentences. Circle the words with —ut**
and write them.

1. Some people have a bad gut feeling about me.

_____

2. It's about time that I got out of this rut.

_____

3. Stop yelling at me! Cut it out! _____

4. I was arrested, but it was a mistake. _____

C. **Write your own sentence.**
Use an —ut word.

_____

_____

D. **Write the —ut words.**

Phonics: Short a
—and
hand

| hand |
| band |
| sand |

A. Read the words in color.
Make other —and words below.

l + and = _____

st + and = _____

B. Read the sentences. Circle the words with —and
and write them.

1. In times of trouble, my family lends me

   a hand. _____

2. In this land, the law will help you. _____

3. I won't lose my job with the band. _____

4. Will they stand by and let the wrong man

   be arrested? _____

C. Write your own sentence.
Use an —and word.

_____

_____

D. Write the —and words.

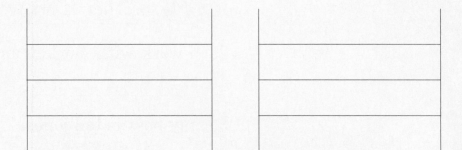

Capitalizing Letters

▶ Dan, Nan, and Jan are lucky.
It's about time that I got lucky.

A. Copy the names.   Start each with a capital letter.

1. Bill _____   2. Jan _____

3. Kent _____   4. Tad Wells _____

5. Pat Key _____   6. Ned Land _____

B. Copy the sentences.   Start with a capital letter.

1. My chances to go home are good.

_____

2. The boss sent my pay home.

_____

3. I won't lose my job.

_____

**C. Mark out the letters that should be capitals.
Write the sentence correctly.**

1. my brother dan works on cars.
   My brother Dan works on cars.

2. i work with pat key and tad wells.

_____

3. my boss is tad jones.

_____

A Good Ending

Well, Ned talked to the woman about me. She looked at me and a man like me. She feels in her gut that she got it wrong.

At times they do arrest people by mistake. The wrong people pay for it. We're with you in this time of trouble. The family will stand by you, Ed.

—Ending—

The woman will talk to the cops about the mistake and get them to let me go. Ned will talk to them and work it out. They'll get the man that looks like me. With luck the man will be arrested and do time for this trouble.

This will have a good ending, and you will win.

—Ending—

I feel bad about being arrested.
But I'll feel good about this man
being in the hands of the law.
I'll feel good about going home!

Think About It

1. What mistake did the woman make?
2. How did Mother feel about it?

Help in Time

# of Trouble

I sit by my dad and talk to him.
I have to yell to talk to him.   On a
stand by the bed are a light and
some water.   Dad isn't well.
My brothers and I feel sad about this.
A nurse helps us out from time to time.

Review Words

A. Check the words you know.

☐ 1. bed   ☐ 2. for   ☐ 3. light

☐ 4. nurse   ☐ 5. sit   ☐ 6. stand

☐ 7. talk   ☐ 8. walk   ☐ 9. water

☐ 10. well   ☐ 11. we're   ☐ 12. yell

B. Read the sentence.

Dad yells for the nurse to get him some water.

C. Write these sentences.

1. Dad yells for the nurse to get him some water.

    _____

2. The nurse will help Dad get well.

    _____

3. I sit by the bed and talk to Dad.

    _____

4. We're helping Dad get out of bed and walk.

    _____

5. The nurse set the water by the light on the stand.

    _____

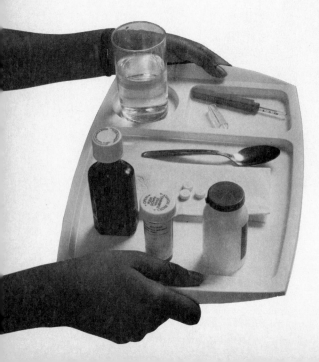

Sight Words

all **did** **lot**

▶ We <u>all</u> <u>did</u> a <u>lot</u> for my dad.

A. Read the words in color. Read the example sentence. Underline the new words in sentences 1–4.

1. We all fed Dad good food in bed.

2. Dad did some walking with help from Jed.

3. Dad likes to use the radio a lot.

4. He has it going all the time.

B. Draw lines to match the words.

all   LOT

did   ALL

lot   DID

C. Write the words below in the sentences.

Did **all** **lot**

1. D__ we do wrong to have Dad at home with us?

2. The nurse likes a__ the work we did.

3. The nurse is a l__ of help to Dad.

D. Write the sentence.

We all did a lot for my dad.

Sight Words

kin   old   age

▶ We're <u>kin</u> and will be with Dad in <u>old</u> <u>age</u>.

A. Read the words in color. Read the example sentence. Underline the new words in sentences 1—4.

1. Kin is family, and this family likes to help Dad.

2. A man the age of Dad can do a lot.

3. Old people like to get out from time to time.

4. The nurse helps Dad walk to her old car.

B. Write the words in the boxes.

kin

old

age

C. Write the words below in the sentences.

age   old   kin

1. Dad likes to talk to people in this a__ group.

2. They talk about good o__ times.

3. We're k__ and are lucky to have a family.

D. Write the sentence.

We're kin and will be with Dad in old age.

Sight Words

laugh   friends   read

▶ **Dad can <u>laugh</u> and <u>read</u> with <u>friends</u>.**

A. Read the words in color. Read the example sentence. Underline the new words in sentences 1–4.

1. Dad met a group of friends.

2. Ned and Jan are good friends to Dad.

3. They all laugh a lot to help Dad get well.

4. They read all the time.

B. Write the three new words into the puzzle.

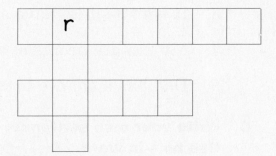

C. Write the words below in the sentences.

friends   laughs   reads

1. Dad and some f _ _ _ _ _ _ go out in the car.

2. Dad l _ _ _ _ _ _ at home with my brothers.

3. He r _ _ _ _ _, eats, and gets to bed feeling good.

D. Write the sentence.

Dad can laugh and read with friends.

_____

Phonics: Short i
—in
kin

kin

pin

tin

win

A. Read the words in color.
Make other —in words below.

b + in = _____

d + in = _____

s + in = _____

B. Read the sentences. Circle the words with —in
and write them.

1. Lin cut her hand on a tin can. _____

    _____

2. The nurse has a pin on her hat. _____

3. It isn't a sin to have a lot of money. _____

4. My kin are people of all ages. _____

5. Dad has a chance to win a radio. _____

C. Write your own sentence.
Use an —in word.

_____

_____

D. Write the —in words.

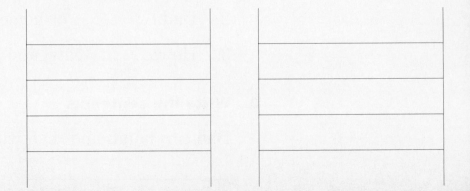

Phonics: Short o
—ot
lot

lot
cot
dot
hot

A. Read the words in color.
Make other —ot words below.

g + ot = _____   n + ot = _____

j + ot = _____   p + ot = _____

B. Read the sentences. Circle the words with —ot and write them.

1. Dad was not feeling well. _____

2. Dad got well with all our help. _____

3. The nurse has a lot of love for sick

    people. _____

4. We fed Dad good hot food. _____

C. Write your own sentence.
Use an —ot word.

_____

_____

D. Write the —ot words.

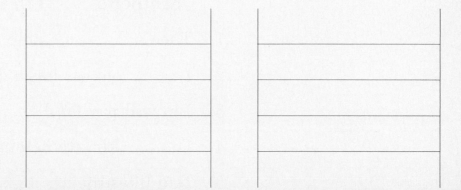

Adding 's to Names

Dad + 's = Dad's bed

(the bed of Dad)

A. Read the words and write them.

1. Dad's kin

2. sister's van

3. nurse's hat

4. family's help

5. Lin's car

6. Jed's work

B. Practice reading the sentences.

Dad's kin are helping him get well. The family's help is good for him. He likes the nurse's help.

Lin's old car has a dent in it. Jed can work on Lin's car. Lin will pay for Jed's work. Jed's work helps Lin, and Lin's work helps Dad.

C. Read these words. Then write one of the words in each sentence.

Jed's   Dad's   nurse's

brother's   Lin's   family's

1. The f _ _ _ _ _ _ help is good for Dad.

2. L _ _ _ old car has a dent in it.

3. Lin will pay for J _ _ _ work.

4. D _ _ _ kin are helping him get well.

5. Dad likes the n _ _ _ _ _ help.

Friends and Kin

Can you lend me a hand with this? I got it for my friend Lin, the nurse. She did a lot for me. She did a lot for all of us.

It isn't a holiday, is it Dad?

It isn't a holiday, but it's about time I did some good for people. This is for Lin's old car.

—Friends—

This is wrong. We did a lot of work for Dad. Helping him get well was a big job! We run to get him fed on time. But it looks like Lin will win Dad's love, not us!

We're Dad's kin—Dad's family. It's our job to help him. Don't be mad. Feel good for him. Let him do this for Lin.

Is all of this for friends, Dad?

You bet! I'm feeling good about people helping me get well. I got lucky. My friends are tops!

—Friends—

Dan, this is for you from me. Jed, this is for you. It's a light, and you can set it on the stand by the bed. This is for you, Nan. You like to read, and this will make you laugh.

You are talking about friends, Dad. We're kin, not friends.

At my old age, Nan, children can be the top friends of all. I'm lucky to have you and Jed and Dan. You helped me get out and walk. You led me to a good group of friends. I'm a lucky man to be in a family like this. People you love are friends, and I love you all.

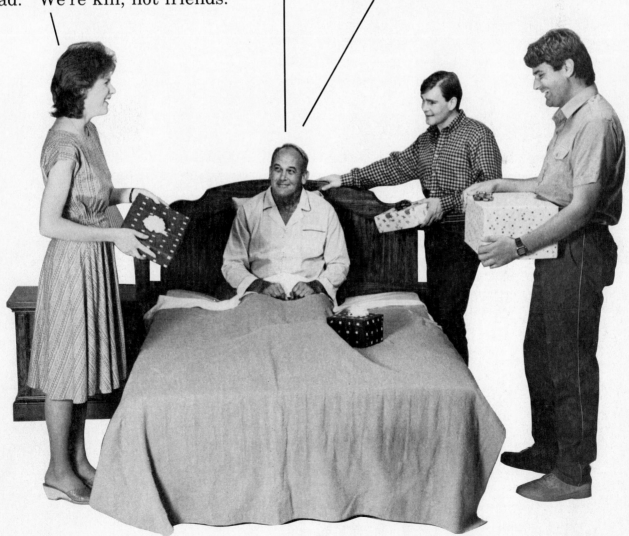

Think About It   1. Who are Dad's kin?   2. How did they help Dad?

A Chance at the Big Time

Mother: You have this going all the time! It makes a din in our home, and I don't like it!

Father: Dan, you have to go out and look for a job. You can't be at home all the time. Do you feel good doing this?

Dan: I get a good feeling doing this. Is it a mistake for me to feel good? Don't be mad about this.

Review Words

A. Check the words you know.

☐ 1. band   ☐ 2. chance   ☐ 3. good

☐ 4. group   ☐ 5. home   ☐ 6. lose

☐ 7. mistake   ☐ 8. mother   ☐ 9. read

☐ 10. this   ☐ 11. time   ☐ 12. trouble

B. Read the sentence.

I have a chance to work with a good group.

C. Write these sentences.

1. The band has a chance to be in the big time.

_____

2. I can't lose my good home.

_____

3. I got in trouble with Mother by mistake.

_____

4. Did you read this about the band?

_____

Sight Words

fit   music   guitar

▶ My <u>guitar</u> <u>music</u> will <u>fit</u> in with the group.

A. **Read the words in color. Read the example sentence. Underline the new words in sentences 1–4.**

1. My dad got me the guitar.

2. I love to make music with a group like this.

3. The music fits my feelings.

4. Can this guitar win me a job in the band?

B. **Write the words in the boxes.**

fit

music

guitar

C. **Write the words below in the sentences.**

music   fit   guitar

1. My m_ _ _ _ isn't some fad for me.

2. I'll f_ _ in with a good group.

3. I'll work at my g_ _ _ _ _ music.

D. **Write the sentence.**

My guitar music will fit in with the group.

Sight Words

son   plays   his

▶ My <u>son</u> <u>plays</u> <u>his</u> guitar.

A. Read the words in color.   Read the example sentence.   Underline the new words in sentences 1–4.

1. Our son plays guitar music all the time.

2. Some of his music has mistakes in it.

3. I got his guitar from our friend Tad.

4. Tad feels that my son will do well in a band.

B. Draw lines to match the words.

son   PLAY

play   HIS

his   SON

C. Write the words below in the sentences.

son   his   play

1. My s__ can play pop music.

2. The band likes h__ work.

3. I'll let his band p___ in our home.

D. Write the sentence.

My son plays his guitar.

Sight Words

fun   father   find

▶ **Will <u>Father</u> <u>find</u> time to have <u>fun</u> with us?**

A. Read the words in color. Read the example sentence. Underline the new words in sentences 1–4.

1. Our band has fun playing in my home.

2. Father got mad at us for being at home all the time.

3. Father did find some time to be with us.

4. We played music that my father likes.

B. Look down and across. Find the words in the box. Circle them.

father

fun

find

j	x	p	k	s	l	u	b
s	t	f	a	t	h	e	r
b	i	u	f	i	n	d	o
n	f	n	o	q	a	e	j

C. Write the words below in the sentences.

father   find   fun

1. My f_____ feels that our band is good.

2. We'll f___ good jobs for our band.

3. A big job can be f__ to do.

D. Write the sentence.

Will Father find time to have fun with us?

Phonics: Short u
—un
fun

fun
run
sun

A. Read the words in color.
Make other —un words below.

b + un = _____

g + un = _____

n + un = _____

B. Read the sentences.   Circle the words with —un and write them.

1.   My band will play out in the sun. _____

2.   This city has laws about guns. _____

3.   Tad has fun playing his guitar. _____

4.   Our dog will run and hop in our

van. _____

5.   Our band played for some nuns. _____

C. Write your own sentence.
Use an —un word.

_____

_____

D. Write the —un words.

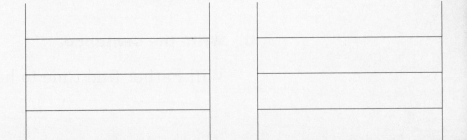

Phonics: Short i
—it
fit

fit

hit

lit

sit

A. Read the words in color.
Make other —it words below.

b + it = _____

k + it = _____

p + it = _____

qu + it = _____

B. Read the sentences. Circle the words with —it and write them.

1. The band can fit our music to age groups.

_____

2. Our band can't quit playing. _____

3. Father will sit by the band. _____

4. With a bit of luck, the band can be a hit.

_____ _____

C. Write your own sentence.
Use an —it word.

_____

_____

D. Write the —it words.

Doubling a Letter To Add —ed and —ing

stop + ed = sto**pped**   stop + ing = sto**pping**

A. **To write the word, double the last letter and add the ending.**

Add —ed:	Add —ing:
1. hop _____	1. let _____
2. stop_____	2. get _____
3. pet _____	3. sit _____
4. fit _____	4. stop_____

B. **Practice reading the sentences.**

My father is mad about my band. He feels that I'm letting the band have all my time. The band had stopped by my home to play. We're getting a good group of people to play. I got Father to stop and look at us. He was sitting by the band. We fitted our music to his age group. He did like our band.

C. **Read these words. Then write one of the words in each sentence.**

sitting	stopped	fitted
letting	getting	stopping

1. We're g_____ a good group to play.

2. I'm l_____ the band have all my time.

3. Father was s_____ by the band.

4. We f_____ our music to his age group.

5. The band had s_____ by my home.

Working Out With the Band

Our band is doing OK, and we're finding jobs. We have fun, but we have a lot of work to do. No band can play well all the time. I've worked a lot at reading music, but I make some mistakes. My guitar music isn't all good. My mother and father both help by letting the band play at our home.

—Band—

Father feels good about me, his son. And he feels that our band will be a big hit. We find music that fits people in all age groups. We play pop music for children and old-time music for some groups. It's a lot of work to find the music people like, but we're getting a lot of chances to play.

—Band—

We talk a lot about our music. Will the band be a hit and have a chance to make the big time? All music is work, but it's work we love. Our music makes people feel good, and we feel good about it. To make the big time, we can't quit. With luck we'll find chances to play the music we love.

Think About It

1. How do Mother and Father help?
2. What age group does the band play for?

UNIT 1 Review

A. Write the words below in the sentences.

lucky	win	on	chance
ticket	lose	hat	home

1. The Key family has a l_____ ticket.

2. The t_____ can pay money.

3. They can w__ with a lucky ticket.

4. You can l___ money o_ a ticket.

B. Write —an or —at to make new words.
Then write each word in a sentence.

1. m + __ = _____   Dan is a _____.

2. f + __ = _____   Dan sits by a _____.

3. h + __ = _____   Pat buys a _____ for Dan.

4. c + __ = _____   I have a fat _____.

C. Add —s to the words.
Write the correct words in the sentences below.

ticket _____   van _____

chance _____   store _____

1. The Keys went to two _____.

2. They stop to buy three lucky _____.

3. They have three _____ to win.

4. They can win _____ with lucky tickets.

UNIT 2 Review

A. Write the words below in the sentences.

my	sent	will
got	mother	love
make	children	went

1. I g___ a job in the city.

2. M_ mother w____ help me tend the c_____ ___.

3. I s____ my l____ to my m_____.

4. I w____ to the city to m____ money.

**B. Write —end or —ent to make new words.
Then write each word in a sentence.**

1. w + ____ = _____   I _____ to the city to work.

2. r + ____ = _____   I _____ my home.

3. s + ____ = _____   I can _____ you a ticket.

4. l + ____ = _____   He will _____ me money.

C. Write the correct words in the sentences.

1. I am _____ in the city.

works
working

2. I have _____ a home.

rents
rented

3. It _____ like I will make it.

looks
looking

4. My mother is _____ us.

helped
helping

UNIT 3 Review

A. Write the words below in the sentences.

smoke	smoking	do
feel	health	bet
out	group	ad

1. I will work to stop s_____.

2. I f____ that I can stop.

3. I went to a h_____ group.

4. I b___ that the group can help me.

B. Write —ad or —et to make new words.
Then write each word in a sentence.

1. g + __ = _____   I will _____ help.

2. y + __ = _____   We did not go _____.

3. h + __ = _____   I _____ to stop smoking.

4. d + __ = _____   My _____ is a good man.

C. Draw lines to match the words.

1. I will   it's

2. they will   can't

3. I am   I'll

4. it is   they'll

5. can not   I'm

UNIT 4 Review

A. Write the words below in the sentences.

our	holiday	fed
be	some	good
eat	talk	top

1. Our family will have a good h_____.

2. We will t____ and eat a lot.

3. I will set the food on t__ of the table.

4. I'll go to the store to get g____ food.

**B. Write —op or —ed to make new words.
Then write each word in a sentence.**

1. f + __ = _____   I _____ my dog.

2. r + __ = _____   The dog food is _____.

3. c + __ = _____   I met a _____.

4. st + __ = _____   We met at a bus _____.

C. Draw lines to match the words.

1. we are   we'll

2. we will   can't

3. is not   we're

4. was not   won't

5. can not   isn't

6. will not   wasn't

UNIT 5 Review

A. Write the words below in the sentences.

trouble	wrong	but
mistake	about	law
arrested	hand	time

1. I got in t_ _ _ _ _ _ by mistake.

2. The cops a_ _ _ _ _ _ _ me, but I did not do it.

3. The law will lend me a helping h_ _ _.

4. It's a_ _ _ _ _ time for me to get out.

B. Write —ut or —and to make new words.
Then write each word in a sentence.

1. c + _ _ = _ _ _ _ _ _ _   I _ _ _ _ _ _ _ my hand.

2. b + _ _ = _ _ _ _ _ _ _   I was sick, _ _ _ _ _ _ _ I'm OK.

3. l + _ _ _ = _ _ _ _ _ _   We can buy some _ _ _ _ _ _ .

4. b + _ _ _ = _ _ _ _ _ _   He plays in a _ _ _ _ _ _ .

C. Mark out the letters that should be capitals.   Write the sentences correctly.

1. my brother dan and i work on cars.

_____

2. jan is my sister and dan is my brother.

_____

3. my boss is ned land.

_____

4. pat key got some money to help me.

_____

UNIT 6 Review

A. Write the words below in the sentences.

all	kin	laugh
did	old	friends
lot	age	read

1. We a___ did a lot for my dad.

2. Dad's kin will be with him in old a___.

3. Dad and I talk and l_____.

4. I r____ to Dad a lot.

B. Write —in or —ot to make new words. Then write each word in a sentence.

1. k + ___ = _____   Dad and I are _____.

2. w + ___ = _____   We'll _____ in the end.

3. l + ___ = _____   I love Dad a _____.

4. n + ___ = _____   Dad is _____ well.

C. Write the correct word in each sentence.

1. Dad likes the _____ help.   nurse
                                              nurse's

_____

2. _____ kin help him get well.   Dad's
                                              Dad

_____

3. _____ car has a big dent.   Lin
                                              Lin's

_____

4. Lin will pay _____ to work on the car.   Jed
                                                 Jed's

_____

UNIT 7 Review

A. Write the words below in the sentences.

fit	music	fun
son	guitar	find
his	father	plays

1. Dan got a guitar for his s___.

2. My f_____ will find time to talk to me.

3. Our band p_____ hit music.

4. We have fun playing our m_____.

B. Write —un or —it to make new words.
Then write each word in a sentence.

1. g + __ = _____   I don't have a _____.

2. r + __ = _____   My dog will _____ with me.

3. qu + __ = _____   I can't _____ the band.

4. h + __ = _____   The band will be a big _____.

C. Write the correct word in each sentence.

1. The band _____ by my home to play.

   stopped
   stopping

2. My dog is _____ and running.

   hopped
   hopping

3. I am _____ my dog.

   petted
   petting

4. We _____ ten guitars into our van.

   fitted
   fitting

Word List

Below is a list of the 165 words that are presented to students in *Book 2* of *Reading for Today*. These words will be reviewed in later books. The numeral following each word refers to the page on which the word is introduced to the students.

A

about 53
ad 29
age 64
all 63
arrested 52

B

bad 30
ban 6
band 55
bat 7
be 39
bend 18
bent 19
bet 28
bin 66
bit 79
bun 78
but 52

C

can't 32
cat 7
chance 5
chances 8
children 16
cop 42
cot 67
cut 54

D

dad 30
dent 19
did 63
din 66
do 27
don't 44
dot 67

E

eat 40
end 18

F

fad 30
fan 6
fat 7
father 77
fed 41

feel 29
find 77
fit 75
fitted 80
friend 65
fun 77

G

getting 80
good 41
got 15
group 28
guitar 75
gun 78
gut 54

H

had 30
hand 53
hat 5
health 28
his 76
hit 79
holiday 39
homes 8
hop 42
hopped 80
hot 67

I

I'll 32
I'm 32
isn't 44
it's 32
I've 44

J

Jed 43
jet 31
jot 67

K

kin 64
kit 79

L

land 55
laugh 65
law 52